BASKETBALL LEGENDS

Kareem Abdul-Jabbar

Charles Barkley

Larry Bird

Wilt Chamberlain

Clyde Drexler

Julius Erving

Patrick Ewing

Anfernee Hardaway

Grant Hill

Magic Johnson

Michael Jordan

Jason Kidd

Reggie Miller

Hakeem Olajuwon

Shaquille O'Neal

Scottie Pippen

David Robinson

Dennis Rodman

CHELSEA HOUSE PUBLISHERS

BASKETBALL LEGENDS

SHAQUILLE O'NEAL

Tim Ungs

Introduction by
Chuck Daly

CHELSEA HOUSE PUBLISHERS
New York • *Philadelphia*

Produced by Daniel Bial and Associates
New York, New York

Picture research by Alan Gottlieb
Cover illustration by Robert Tanenbaum

3 5 7 9 8 6 4

Library of Congress Cataloging-in-Publication Data

Ungs, Tim
     Shaquille O'Neal / Tim Ungs.
        p. cm.—(Basketball legends)
     Includes bibliographical references and index.
     ISBN 0-7910-2437-7
     1. O'Neal, Shaquille—Juvenile literature. 2. Basketball players—
United States—Biography—Juvenile literature. I. Title.
II. Series.
GV884.054U54   1996
796.323'092—dc20

                                     [B]95-9263
                                        CIP
                                        AC

CONTENTS

BECOMING A
BASKETBALL LEGEND 6
CHUCK DALY

Chapter 1
LIKE A HOUSE FALLING IN ON YOU 9

Chapter 2
LITTLE WARRIOR 19

Chapter 3
GET OUT OF THE WAY! 25

Chapter 4
GOING TO THE MOUNTAIN 33

Chapter 5
A WHOLE NEW BALL GAME 43

Chapter 6
BUILDING A HOUSE ON
LEGENDS LANE 53

CHRONOLOGY 61
STATISTICS 62
FURTHER READING 63
INDEX 64

BECOMING A
BASKETBALL LEGEND

Chuck Daly

What does it take to be a basketball superstar? Two of the three things it takes are easy to spot. Any great athlete must have excellent skills and tremendous dedication. The third quality needed is much harder to define, or even put in words. Others call it leadership or desire to win, but I'm not sure that explains it fully. This third quality relates to the athlete's thinking process, a certain mentality and work ethic. One can coach athletic skills, and while few superstars need outside influence to help keep them dedicated, it is possible for a coach to offer some well-time words in order to keep that athlete fully motivated. But a coach can do no more than appeal to a player's will to win; how much that player is then capable of ensuring victory is up to his own internal workings.

In recent times, we have been fortunate to have seen some of the best to play the game. Larry Bird, Magic Johnson, and Michael Jordan had all three components of superstardom in full measure. The brought their teams to numerous championships, and made the players around them better. (They also made their coaches look smart.)

I myself coached a player who belongs in that class, Isiah Thomas, who helped leader the Detroit Pistons to consecutive NBA crowns. Isiah is not tall—he's just over six feet—but he could do whatever he wanted with the ball. And what he wanted to do most was lead and win.

All the players I mentioned above and those whom this series will chronicle are tremendously gifted athletes, but for the most part, you can't play professional basketball at all unless you have excellent skills. And few players get to stay on their team unless they are willing to dedicate themselves to improving their talents even more, learning about their opponents, and finding a way to join with their teammates and win.

It's that third element that separates the good player from the superstar, the memorable players from the legends of the game. Superstars known when to take over the game. If the situation calls for a defensive stop, the superstars stand up and do it. If the situation calls for a big shot, they want the ball. They don't want the ball simply because of their own glory or ego. Instead they know—and their teammates know—that they are the ones who can deliver, regardless of the pressure.

The words "legend" and "superstar" are often tossed around without real meaning. Taking a hard look at some of those who truly can be classified as "legends" can provide insight into the things that brought them to that level. All of them developed their legacy over numerous season of play, even if certain games will always stand out in the memories of those who saw them. Those games typically featured amazing feats of all-around play. No matter how great the fans thought the superstars, the players were capable yet of surprising them, their opponents, and occasionally even themselves. The desire to win took over, and with their dedication and athletic skills already in place, they were capable of the most astonishing achievements.

CHUCK DALY, most recently the head coach of the New Jersey Nets, guided the Detroit Pistons to two straight NBA championships, in 1989 and 1990. He earned a gold medal as coach of the 1992 U.S. Olympic basketball team—the so-called "Dream Team"—and was inducted into the Pro Basketball Hall of Fame in 1994.

1

LIKE A HOUSE FALLING IN ON YOU

On February 20, 1993, at its annual All-Star Game in Salt Lake City, the National Basketball Association (NBA) found itself in a state of transition. After more than a decade of unprecedented success, broken attendance records, and outstanding television ratings, the league was suddenly short on superstars.

The year before, two of the best players of all time, Larry Bird of the Boston Celtics and Earvin "Magic" Johnson of the Los Angeles Lakers, had retired. While no one was surprised when Bird announced that the excruciating pain in his back had at last become too much for him, Magic's announcement stunned the world—he was retiring from basketball after learning that he had tested positive for HIV, the virus that causes AIDS.

Michael Jordan, the league's top drawing card, was still around, of course, but no one was sure for how long. The NBA's best player

---

In his rookie season, Shaq was named a starter in the All-Star game—the first person so honored since Michael Jordan.

My shoe contract is bigger than your shoe contract! Patrick Ewing (right) had been the starting center for the East in the All-Star game, until Shaq came along.

had been hinting for some time that the long season was wearing him down. Feeling he had nothing left to prove, throughout the 1992-93 season Jordan made it clear that he would be retiring sooner rather than later. After leading the Chicago Bulls to their third consecutive championship, he made good on his word and announced he would not be returning for the following season. (Jordan's retirement ended suddenly after 21 months, when he gave up on his dream of becoming a professional baseball player and rejoined the Bulls for the playoff drive in the 1994-95 season.) So, while no one in Salt Lake City knew it at the time, this was to be Jordan's last All-Star Game appearance for at least two years.

Was there any young basketball player ready to wear their shoes?

It's hard to imagine now, but in 1979, when Bird and Magic were drafted into the NBA, the league was struggling. With players like Julius Erving and Kareem Abdul-Jabbar, the NBA was not without its marquee attractions, but in general fans thought the season was too long, that most players were only interested in showing off or padding their own statistics, and didn't give their best effort to win night after night. Even the NBA Finals were far from being the prime-time television attraction that they are now. Compared to professional baseball and football, basketball was a second-rate sport and, at the close of the 1970s, as many as six teams were on the verge of going out of business.

With their flair for the dramatic, team-first attitude, and intense rivalry, Bird and Magic changed all that. They brought to NBA basketball a sense of excitement and fan appeal that it had never had before, and when Michael Jordan came along six years later, he elevated the league to an even higher plane. For nine years in a row, from 1983-84 to 1991-92, the NBA's Most Valuable Player was either Larry Bird, Magic Johnson, or Michael Jordan. Each won the MVP award three times, and 13 out of the last 14 NBA finals had featured one, if not two, of the game's three premier stars. They had style, class, and were, above all, winners. Each of them had at least three NBA championship rings to prove it.

Today the NBA is among the richest and most glamorous sports leagues in the world, a billion-dollar global business—thanks in no small part to the contributions of these three players. Larry, Magic, and Michael—no last names were needed—seemed impossible to replace. The NBA was facing the end of an era, and its leaders could be forgiven for thinking no upcoming star had the personality and game to make people forget the departing stars.

So on February 20 it was no surprise that all eyes were on the one rookie who had caused more excitement than any player had caused in years. At 7'1" and 303 pounds, he also happened to be the biggest All-Star and, at twenty, the youngest player ever to appear in the NBA's annual showcase. It didn't matter that nearly every big name in basketball was in Salt Lake City, Utah, even many all-time greats who were there for an NBA Legends exhibition game. "This year," wrote a reporter for the New York Times, "the All-Star Weekend is basically the Shaquille O'Neal Show."

Shaquille O'Neal—the Shaq—of the Orlando Magic, the starting center for the Eastern Conference squad, had already made a strong impression on the fans when, just a few weeks before the All-Star Game, he brought down an entire backboard and basket structure with a mighty slam dunk. It was the Shaq's first professional game on national TV, against Charles Barkley and the Phoenix Suns, and the first chance for a national television audience to see him play. Not many people remembered that the Suns beat the Magic that day, but no one could forget the awesome power Shaq showed with his legendary dunk just two minutes and twenty-seven seconds into the game. As an advertisement for the upcoming All-Star Game, the timing was perfect—so perfect that some even thought it was a publicity stunt. Fans from coast to coast were making a point of tuning in to see how the 300-pound man-child would stand up to the NBA's best.

The Shaq was a genuine rookie sensation. He was so popular that, during the season, the Magic had to arrange a press conference just for him in each of the 25 cities they visited. On All-Star Weekend he was even more in demand, and seemed to be enjoying all the attention. At a charity auction on Friday, one of his jerseys was bought for $55,000. In comparison, a Michael Jordan jersey went for a mere $25,000.

The All-Star game was a good chance for O'Neal to meet and play with other stars such as Larry Johnson.

On Saturday, Shaquille appeared at an NBA "Stay-in-School Jam" and got on stage with his favorite rap group, Fu Schnickens, to perform a song he had done with them on "Arsenio" a few months earlier. "He's got it all," said Magic Johnson, who had worked out with Shaq in the off-season and was more than impressed by what he saw. "He's got the smile, and the talent, and the charisma. And"—referring to the rookie's $40 million contract and lucrative product endorsement deals—"he's sure got the money too."

But while the fans and the press oohed and ahhed over Shaq's dunks and raps, NBA players knew that baskets had been brought down

O'Neal got an elbow in the chest while stopping Karl Malone of the hometown Utah Jazz during first quarter action in the 1993 game.

before. Darryl Dawkins was famous for shattering backboards in the late 1970s, but was in the long run no more than a cartoon-like footnote to basketball history. And while a rapping basketball player was a novelty, rapping was just talk, after all. Opposing centers like Patrick Ewing, David Robinson, and Hakeem Olajuwon wanted to see what that player could do on the floor.

Clearly, Shaquille O'Neal certainly had the personality of a superstar, but the big question was: did he have a game to match it? What had he done to become the first rookie selected to start in the All Star game since Michael Jordan?

The answer was plenty.

At the time of the announcement that he had won the All-Star fan balloting, Shaquille ranked 8th in the league in scoring, with 23.7 points per game, second in rebounding (14.2 per game) and field goal percentage (57.2%), and third in blocked shots, with nearly four per game. Largely due to his presence, the Magic, an expansion team that had only won 21 of 82 games the previous year, was in the thick of a playoff race at midseason.

Shaquille had wasted no time in taking the

NBA by storm. In his first week in the league, he won Player of the Week honors. Not Rookie of the Week. Player. The best in the league, right from day one. No rookie, not even Michael Jordan, had ever done that before.

Combining overwhelming strength with quick footwork and explosive leaping ability, the Shaq could already back the NBA's strongest centers deep into the lane, turn and throw down a mighty dunk, or spin quickly in the opposite direction to bank the shot home. What's more, he could run up and down the court as fast as a small forward, was a good ball handler, and was perfectly willing to throw his enormous body to the floor to recover a loose ball. Particularly fearsome when trailing on the fast break, the Shaq made even the toughest NBA player think twice about trying to stand in front of him to take the charge for an offensive foul.

"When you're seven feet tall you're supposed to have some limitations," said Sam Bowie, who played center for the New Jersey Nets at the time. "But with Shaq I just haven't seen any."

"You don't realize how talented he is until you play against him," said Rony Seikaly, then of the Miami Heat, who had the honor of being the first center to play against Shaq in an NBA exhibition game, and was the first to face him in the regular season. "When he backs into you," said Seikaly, a muscular and aggressive player himself, "it's like a house falling in on you."

The All-Star Game is traditionally a run-and-gun affair, a showcase for players' offensive skills, with very little effort usually given on the defensive end. But the Salt Lake City game was different. Shaquille, along with the other starters on the Eastern Conference All-Stars—

Michael Jordan, Scottie Pippen, Larry Johnson, and Isiah Thomas—found themselves up against a West squad that included Charles Barkley, Clyde Drexler, Hakeem Olajuwon, David Robinson, and two hometown favorites, John Stockton and Karl Malone of the Utah Jazz. One of the most exciting All-Star Games ever, this contest was hard fought from the opening tap, with the lead changing hands fifteen times, and neither team ever trailing by more than nine points.

The Western Conference players challenged Shaquille, and Malone and Robinson were even able to block his shot early on. But Shaquille showed that his game was about more than dunking by draining a fifteen-foot jump shot, and, not being one to disappoint the fans, shook the basket with a couple of monster slams. "I got off to a quick start," he said later, "and felt in the rhythm of the game from the beginning." He made 4 of 9 shots, and scored 13 points in 14 minutes while pulling down 7 rebounds before half-time.

But after half-time, he found himself watching from the bench, as Eastern Conference coach Pat Riley went with Patrick Ewing, the center for his team, the New York Knicks, for most of second half. While Shaquille had beaten Ewing by nearly 300,000 votes in the fan balloting, and was ahead of Ewing in scoring, rebounding, shooting percentage, and blocked shots, Riley called it "ridiculous" that the fans had voted for a first-year player over his seasoned veteran.

Shaquille showed his maturity by refusing to be drawn into the brewing controversy. "The fans put me here and I'm just glad I'm here and

I'm just going to go in the game and have a good time," he said when asked before the game about Riley's comments. He even found a way to have fun with the situation, to demonstrate his poise and sense of humor. When asked if he would have voted for himself to start in front of Ewing, he answered, "Definitely. Shaq is a good player. He dominates and dunks hard. And he's a nice guy."

In the end the West—led by co-MVPs Stockton and Malone—finally pulled it out in overtime, 135-132. While Shaq did get back in the game for the end of the fourth quarter and some of the overtime, he only ended up playing 25 of 53 total minutes—the same as Ewing. Shaquille confessed in his autobiography that he had been stung by Riley's decision, but after the game he again showed his maturity and said only this to the press: "I had fun and I wasn't upset. And I'll tell you something else. Shaq will be back."

That was an understatement. Shaquille O'Neal would indeed be back—as the starting center for the Eastern Conference the next year. The NBA's next superstar had arrived on center stage. The Shaq Attaq had only just begun.

2

LITTLE WARRIOR

It was anything but a straight road to the All-Star Game for Shaquille Rashaun O'Neal. Before Orlando and Salt Lake City, he had lived a nomadic existence, moving every couple of years, living in a number of different places. His three-year stay at Louisiana State University, where he played college ball, was the longest he had been in one place since early childhood. Before coming to Baton Rouge, Shaquille and his family lived in San Antonio, Texas, where he attended high school, and before that on a series of military bases both in the United States and West Germany. But the Shaq story had its beginning in Newark, New Jersey, where he was born on March 6, 1972.

"To me, just by having a name that means something makes you special," said Shaquille's mother, Lucille O'Neal Harrison, who explains that Shaquille Rashaun is an Islamic name that

According to Marcia Davis, who taught Shaquille's fifth-grade class at Fort Stewart Elementary School, he was just like all other kids.

When Shaquille was growing up in and near Newark, New Jersey, National Guardsmen had to patrol the streets after riotings and lootings.

means "Little Warrior." Shaquille's biological father abandoned his family, and Shaquille considers Philip Harrison, who married Lucille when Shaquille was two, to be his true father. Shaquille told an interviewer in 1994, "When my mother needed someone 21 years ago, Phil Harrison was the man. He is my dad. He is the one who raised me and made me what I am today." Shaquille wrote a rap on the subject called "Biological Didn't Bother" for his second album, *Shaq-Fu, the Return.*

When Shaquille was born, both his parents worked for the city of Newark: Philip in the violations bureau, and Lucille in payroll. At the time Newark was recovering from a series of destructive race riots just a few years before, and Shaquille remembered that "the saying was, if you concentrated real hard, you could still smell the smoke from all the fires." Because opportunities in Newark were limited, Philip Harrison joined the army to make a better life for his family, and for a time worked three jobs at once. After putting in a full week at his army job as a supply sergeant, he would drive trucks back and forth between New Jersey and New York City, and would also take on extra work shining shoes or selling hats. Lucille kept the house, cooked, and looked after Shaquille, his younger sisters LaTeefah and Ayesha, and his younger brother Jamal.

When Shaquille was of school age the family moved to Jersey City, and then to an army base in Bayonne, New Jersey. Army base life was to be a constant for most of Shaquille's life, and he found the frequent moves difficult at first: "The worst part was the traveling," he recalled in his autobiography. "Meeting people, getting tight with them, and then having to leave. Sometimes when you came into a new place they tested you. I was teased a lot—teased about my name, teased about my size, teased about being flunked in school because I was so big. Because of that I got in a lot of fights and it sometimes took me a while to make new friends."

Yet Shaquille came to learn that there were many positives to balance the negatives of growing up in the army. "You learn things as an army brat that you don't even know you're learning. The discipline, for one thing. If you screw up—and man, did I screw up—you face the consequences. With my dad, there was no, 'Well, we'll let it go this time.' He didn't let anything go. And gradually, you learn how to behave, how to respect authority. Also, I think service kids are a little more socially aware than other kids. We made friends easier and quicker and adapted to new situations, simply because we had to. It was a survival tool."

When Shaquille was in the sixth grade, the family moved to Fulda, West Germany. Shaquille, who admits that in his youth he was "sort of a juvenile delinquent," became even more unruly after the move. "The rumor among army kids in Germany was that if your parents couldn't handle you, they'd send you back to the States. I hated Germany at first, so I did everything in my power to make my father send

Dale Brown was instrumental in helping Shaquille along, starting when Shaquille was only 13 years old.

me back." But his father made it clear that he would never send him back, and that every time Shaquille stepped out of line, he could look forward to more discipline.

Thanks to his parents' constant attentions and his discovery of sports, Shaq was able to put his misbehaving ways behind him. Shaquille remembers vividly the day his father "took me aside, shoved a basketball in my face, and said: 'You see this ball? You take care of this ball, you love this ball, you sleep with this ball, you dream with this ball. Because someday this ball is going to put food on your table.'"

Shaquille credits his father, his first and perhaps his toughest coach, with teaching him the fundamentals of the game. Philip Harrison stood 6'5", weighed 250 pounds, and took pride in the fact that he had gotten his teeth knocked out by Boston Celtics star Dave Cowens in a pickup game in East Orange, New Jersey. He was as demanding as he was tough. "He wanted me to block shots like a Bill Russell, rebound and make the outlet pass like a Wes Unseld, score like a Wilt [Chamberlain] or Kareem [Abdul-Jabbar], handle the ball like an Oscar Robertson or a Jerry West." While young Shaquille at first found it difficult to play up to his father's expectations, he later realized that the point his father stressed from the beginning "was to be versatile instead of one-dimensional, to impose my will on every part of the game every minute I was on the floor. That advice I took to heart."

Shaquille had found his calling. "The more I practiced basketball, the better I got, and the further it kept me away from trouble. My father's lessons were simple: work hard, concentrate, be mentally tough, be persistent. His work ethic, the kind of person he was, came through in the way he coached me in sports." But Shaquille's success did not come overnight. As a freshman in high school in Germany, Shaquille was not even good enough to make the basketball team on the army base, even though he already was 6'8". At his father's urging, he attended a clinic given by Dale Brown, the coach of the Louisiana State University Tigers. After the clinic Shaquille approached Brown and asked for some advice about a weight program so he could develop his legs and learn how to dunk.

"How long you been in the army, soldier?" Brown asked.

"I'm not in the army," Shaquille said. "I'm only thirteen."

He couldn't believe it. "You're on the high school basketball team?" he asked.

"No, I'm not good enough." Shaquille replied.

That was too much for Coach Brown. "Where's your father?" he said.

Shaquille's father immediately made it clear to Coach Brown that he would not be won over by the standard college basketball recruiting speech. "Coach, I'm not trying to be rude," he told him. "But I'm not all that interested in hearing about basketball." Not long after Shaquille attended Brown's clinic, Sergeant Harrison was transferred again, this time back to the United States, to San Antonio, Texas.

3
GET OUT OF THE WAY!

"**S**an Antonio (Texas) was where I first made my mark in the basketball world," Shaquille recalled. "It was all struggles up until then." At fifteen Shaquille entered Robert C. Cole Junior and Senior High School, as a junior, in the fall of 1987. Because the student body at Cole was composed mostly of the children of service people and Department of Defense employees, "it wasn't anything strange," wrote Shaquille, "when a black kid who had spent several years in Germany suddenly showed up in September. Of course, when a seven-foot black kid shows up, that was cause for some curiosity."

Shaquille loved high school. He worked hard and got good grades, "mostly A's and B's, rarely a C or D." One of the extracurricular activities Shaquille enjoyed was keeping stats for the football team, which he did both years he was at Cole. Shaq wrote that the football coach saw it as "a good psychological weapon. The other

O'Neal led his Cole High School team to the 1989 Texas state championship.

team would show up, and they'd introduce me, and they'd say, 'Man, that kid's the statistician? How big are the players?'"

In the two years since the Dale Brown clinic, Shaquille's coordination had caught up with his size and all of his hard work was beginning to pay off. A year earlier, when he couldn't even make his high school team in Germany, he was told: "You should be a goalie in soccer. You're too slow, you've got too big feet, and you're too clumsy." Back in the U.S. for his junior year, not only did Shaquille make the high school team, he was without question its star. Though still nowhere near his potential, he was a player who was beginning to attract attention, as well as double- and triple-teams from every opponent Cole faced. Shaquille led Cole High to an undefeated regular season record, but his team's one loss came in the Texas State Class 2A Regional Finals. Shaquille had 4 fouls in the first quarter of that game against Liberty Hills, and missed two crucial free throws with five seconds left. "I felt terrible," he wrote, "as terrible as I had ever felt about anything up to . . . that point." Cole High finished with 32 wins and 1 loss, and Shaquille returned for his senior season determined to lead his team to the state championship.

Herb More, an assistant to Cole's head coach Dave Madura, told writer Bill Gutman that "Shaquille was one of the hardest workers on the team. Whether on the court or in the weight room, he always gave me the feeling that he wanted to improve all the time, wanted to be the best in everything he did."

More thought that Lucille Harrison should get some of the credit. "I think his mother had a very positive effect on him," More said. "She isn't mentioned as much as his father, but she was a real stabilizing force with him. His dad is military and has a more hard-line, brusque manner about him. His mom is strong but quiet, and I think he gets that from her. Shaquille was always real soft-spoken." (Shaquille's father himself readily concedes that Lucille has had more clout in the family than most people think. "Everybody's got this myth that, when the sergeant speaks, everybody listens," he told a reporter from the *New York Times*, but, he said, pointing to his wife, "When she speaks, everybody listens.")

More had given up a head coaching job at another school to be an assistant at Cole for the once-in-a-lifetime chance to work closely with a player of Shaquille's promise. At 6'6", with some college ball behind him, Cole would often guard Shaquille in practice. "Basically, all I did was foul him to death," More recalled. "I would get him mad intentionally, and he would complain about it all the time. But my answer was simple. I asked him what he thought our opponents were going to do to him in the games. Then he would nod because he knew I was right."

Shaquille later realized that, as late as his junior year, he was "still kind of a soft player. I still couldn't get that mentality to turn around and try to rip the rim off. My model at the time was actually Dominique Wilkins because of the way he made you go, 'Ooh, look at that!' But I shouldn't have been trying to be an 'ooh, look at that!' kind of player. I needed to be a 'Whoa! Get the heck out of the way!' type of player."

When asked by a reporter what the secret to Cole High's success would be for 1988-89, his senior year, Shaquille answered, "The secret is me." But by now Shaquille, nearly seven feet tall and approaching 270 pounds, was anything but a secret. He had become one of the most sought after high school players in the country. After playing in a summer tournament in Arizona between his junior and senior years, he recalled coming home to find "letters and brochures from all kinds of colleges. I didn't know what had happened. 'Mom,' I said, 'how many places did you write to?' And she said, 'I didn't do anything, son. They just arrived.'"

The Cole coaching staff, like Shaquille's father, emphasized well-rounded play. "We told everyone if you're in the middle on the break, handle the ball," said More. "We wanted everyone to develop an all-around game. Shaquille was fully capable of getting a rebound and taking it coast to coast. He could go all the way for a slam, throw a no-look pass, or pull up and take a fifteen-foot jumper. And he did that in all of our games at one time or another."

Opponents did what they could to stop Shaquille, who because of his size, found it difficult to get favorable calls from officials. "The thing that frustrated me was that I was allowed to be pushed, but I couldn't push back." After repeatedly being hammered in the low post, he began to anticipate the contact and started missing easy shots close to the basket. One day, More recalled, "We were playing in a tournament game up in Marble Falls . . . and the other team was holding Shaquille every time he went up, just hanging all over him. The referees weren't calling anything, so we all started yelling to him, 'Go up and just slam the sucker.' Next time he got the ball he just powered up and dunked.

After that he began slamming everything. No more lay-ups on passes under the basket. From that point on he always went all the way."

For Shaquille's senior year, there was no stopping him, and Cole went undefeated and won the Texas 3A State Championship. While he was without question the main man for Cole, Shaquille also knew what it took to win games, even if it meant giving up the ball. In one game against the defending state champions, he scored only 4 points, but blocked numerous shots and passed the ball when opposing players closed in on him, setting up easy baskets for his teammates. In the title game against Clarksville High, Shaquille overcame foul trouble to score 19 points and rip down 26 rebounds. His statistics for the year— 32.1 points, 22 rebounds, and 8 blocked shots per game—were even more impressive for the fact that many of Cole's victories were blowouts, and Shaquille watched from the bench as substitutes played the fourth quarter of many games.

Shaquille made the *Parade* High School All-

As a teenager, O'Neal showed unusual versatility, not only shooting, rebounding, and blocking, but also in handling the ball.

America team, and was named the Most Valuable Player in two prestigious post season tournaments, the McDonald's All-Star Classic and the Dapper Dan Classic. Unlike most high school superstars, however, there was no suspense about where he would be attending college. Although he considered the University of North Carolina, North Carolina State University, Illinois University, and the University of Arizona, he signed a national letter of intent before his senior season to attend LSU and be reunited with Coach Dale Brown. It was important to Shaquille that LSU's campus in Baton Rouge was close enough to San Antonio so that his parents could drive to see him play at home games. Shaquille also liked the weather there, and preferred the style of play in LSU's conference, the Southeastern Athletic Conference (the SEC). "I looked at it as a big, tough, roughneck, countryboy conference, not like the ACC [the Atlantic Coast Conference] which was kind of the pretty, rich-boy conference."

Of course a big reason for his attending LSU was Coach Brown himself. As he had promised to do in Germany, Brown had kept in touch with Shaquille and his family. Craig Carse, one of Brown's assistant coaches, spent so much time at Cole High recruiting Shaquille he sometimes slept on the couch in the Cole athletic director's office. Shaquille also appreciated the fact that LSU was straightforward and honest in dealing with his family. "In one of the first conversations Dale Brown ever had with my family, my father told him: 'The first person who offers us something illegal is going to get kicked out of our house on his butt.'" Needless to say, everything with LSU was completely on the level.

While many assumed that Philip Harrison chose LSU for his son, the decision was in fact made entirely by Shaquille. "We pushed the boat away the day he decided to go there," Sergeant Harrison recalled. "It was time for him to apply the things we had taught him and the things he had learned in life and to do what he had to do." Next stop: Baton Rouge.

4

GOING TO THE
MOUNTAIN

When Shaquille entered Louisiana State University in the Fall of 1989, he came with more on his mind than basketball. He was there to learn as well. "We want him to get an education so he doesn't need basketball," his father had said, and Shaquille, as always, took his father's words to heart and hit the books hard. "I always went to my study halls and arranged with my professors to make up work while I was away," he said in his autobiography. "People don't realize how tough it is to play basketball and stay on top of your work. Unlike football or baseball, basketball goes across both semesters, and you're gone, sometimes, for a week at a time." In spite of these obstacles, Shaquille had a 2.9 grade point average (out of a possible 4.0) in his first year, the best on the LSU basketball team.

Although he was coming to LSU as a highly

Christian Laettner of Duke University was one of college basketball's biggest stars. But here he stands out of the way as O'Neal goes strong to the hoop.

prized recruit, Shaquille would not be the star of the team in his first year. That honor would certainly belong to sophomore point guard Chris Jackson, who would move on to an NBA career under the name of Mahmoud Abdul-Rauf the very next season. The Tigers also had another seven-footer, Stanley Roberts, who, though not as athletic as Shaquille, at the time had a more advanced offensive game. In his first collegiate season, Shaquille shared the spotlight with his teammates.

LSU was known for fans who were so vocal in their support for the Tigers that the Pete Maravich Assembly Center, the team's home arena, became known as the Deaf Zone because of the noise created by 13,479 Tiger fanatics cheering their team on. With LSU having made it to the NCAA tournament's Final Four twice in the past decade, the LSU fans were used to winning, and they had high hopes for this Tigers team. So, it appeared, did the national media. In a preseason edition, *Sport* magazine ranked LSU the Number 1 team in the country, ahead of perennial basketball powerhouses like the University of Michigan, the University of Nevada at Las Vegas (UNLV), Georgetown University, Duke University, and North Carolina. For a team that had never played together, that was a lot to live up to.

Coach Brown opted for a "Twin Towers" approach, and played both seven-footers on the court at the same time, with Roberts moving to the power forward slot, and Shaquille playing in the pivot. His main responsibilities were to rip down rebounds and block shots, and not to think all that much about scoring. Because of his size and quickness, Jackson played the point guard position, but he was a shooting guard at heart, and looked to score at every opportunity. In one game, against the University of Texas, Jackson scored 51 points, an amazing total against a quality NCAA Division 1 opponent. But it was during that game, when most fans were concentrating on Jackson, that Craig Carse thought he saw a glimmer of what Shaquille would become. "One of the Texas players took a shot from close in, and Shaquille went up and blocked it. He was up so high that it looked as if his armpit was up over the rim. One of our guys got the ball, and Shaquille immediately sprinted downcourt. He cut to the hoop and took a pass, which he just kind of cuffed in his hand and in one motion just went over everybody and dunked it down. It really showed what he was all about."

Shaquille had his ups and downs in his first season, as did the Tigers as a team. While not playing quite up to their number one ranking, LSU had an extremely successful season, including a 107-105 victory over eventual national champion UNLV, a team led by future NBA star Larry Johnson. In that game, while Jackson was torching the UNLV defense for 35 points, Shaquille was controlling the paint with 19 points and 14 rebounds. Another highlight of Shaquille's freshman year came when he blocked 12 shots and had 24 rebounds in a victory over a highly regarded Loyola Marymount team and their star Hank Gathers. In the NCAA tournament, the Tigers advanced to the second round with a victory over Villanova University, only to fall to Georgia Tech and their stars, Kenny Anderson and Dennis Scott.

The Tigers' record in Shaquille's first year

was 23 wins and 9 losses. It had been a very good year, but not quite good enough to satisfy the high hopes of the LSU fans. Shaquille's personal statistics were, however, enough to make them look forward with anticipation to the next season. He averaged 13.9 points, 12.0 rebounds, and 6 blocked shots per game. Both his rebounding and blocked shot totals were first in the SEC. He would have to work on controlling his aggressiveness—he had fouled out of 9 games—and his free-throw shooting, which was only 55.6%, but everyone expected him to build on his promising first year. And he would have to: with Jackson skipping his last two years of college eligibility for the NBA and Roberts leaving the team because of academic problems, Shaquille would be the main man for LSU in his sophomore year.

Between seasons Shaquille worked out with Bill Walton, who many regard as the most dominant collegiate player ever. While he did not quite match his college success in his pro career, Walton still managed, in spite of chronic and painful foot injuries, to lead the Portland Trail Blazers to the NBA title in 1976-77, and was an important part of the Boston Celtics' 1985-86 championship season. Interestingly, Walton compared Shaquille to a forward, not another center, noting that he saw a lot of Charles Barkley in his game. Shaquille, Walton said, "has that quick unrestrainable explosion, like Barkley. It's a raw power you don't get in the weight room. It comes from somewhere else, deep in the soul. This guy may have the physical talent and personal discipline to be the best."

There are some seven-footers who, even if

they could barely leap eight inches, would still help their team. Bill Laimbeer, for example, had a long and effective NBA career with virtually no vertical jump whatsoever. It was said that you could barely slide a piece of paper beneath his feet when he was airborne. Now imagine this: Shaquille's vertical leap improved by eight inches between his first two years to more than 28 inches. He could now jump straight up to touch a spot on the backboard two and a half feet above the rim. He was in terrific physical shape and ready to be the driving force of the LSU squad in his second season.

The Tigers' first big challenge was playing the Arizona Wildcats on the road, who at the time were the second-ranked team in the country. The Wildcats' front line of future NBA players Chris Mills, Sean Rooks, and Brian Williams was known as "the Tucson Skyline," but Shaquille went into their house and dominated the game, scoring 29 points, ripping down 14 rebounds, and blocking 6 shots in a big upset victory. "The tapes don't do him justice," said Mills after the game. "It's kind of amazing to see him in person." Right after that he scored 53 points against Arkansas State University, the only team in his entire college career that chose to guard him with one man and not double-team him. Later in the season, after a victory

Chris Jackson was a teammate of O'Neal's at LSU and later went on to star in the NBA under the name of Mahmoud Abdul-Rauf.

over SEC rival University of Georgia, he won the admiration of their coach Hugh Durham, who said, "Trying to stop Shaquille is a joke. Last year you could play behind him and know he wasn't going to get the ball from those other guys. Now you have to front or side him, and he muscles you out of the lane anyway. They just keep going to the mountain, going to the mountain. Shaq may be unguardable."

Jamal Mashburn, the University of Kentucky star, said that he thought Shaquille was "just another player" before his team played the Tigers. In two games, which the teams split, Shaquille had 61 points and 33 rebounds, moving Mashburn to amend his opinion of the LSU center. "Shaq," Mashburn said, "belongs in a higher league."

Shaquille made a further claim to that status when, during a game against McNeese State University, he had all of Louisiana talking with a breathtakingly spectacular slam. "I was running down the lane trailing the fast break," he recalled, "when I took a missed shot, windmill-dunked it and at the same time jumped completely over a 6'5" guy named Melvin Johnson. Down in Baton Rouge they still just call that The Dunk."

Late in the year, Shaquille suffered a broken leg, a hairline fracture just below the knee, and the Tigers, playing without their leader, lost the season finale and were eliminated in the first round of the SEC tournament. For the opening-round game in the NCAA tournament, Shaquille bravely returned to action, broken leg and all, and had 27 points and 16 rebounds in a heroic losing effort against a very good University of Connecticut team.

Shaquille was a consensus first-team All-American for 1990-91, and was named the SEC Player and Athlete of the Year. The Associated Press, United Press International, and *Sports Illustrated* chose him as Player of the Year, and he was the Tanqueray World Amateur Athlete of the Year. He had averaged 27.6 points, 14.7 rebounds (best in the nation), had 140 blocked shots, a national record for sophomores, and shot nearly 63% from the floor. He became the first player to lead the SEC in scoring, rebounding, field goal percentage, and blocked shots. He even brought his free-throw shooting percentage up to 63.8%. The only statistics that went down were his grades, which slipped a little to a 2.0 GPA. "Too much Nintendo," Shaquille joked, but by next year he had his grades up again, almost to Dean's List standard.

If Shaquille had chosen to, he could have gone straight to the NBA after his sophomore year, and many thought he would have been the number one pick in the draft. He considered leaving college to turn pro, but as he recalled, his father convinced him to return to LSU for another season. "When I was thinking about coming out after my sophomore year my father asked me why. 'To make money,' I said. 'Not good enough,' he said." Shaquille remained a Tiger for one more year.

The 1991-92 season was a difficult one for Shaquille. "My junior year was more bad chemistry, too many egos, too much what's-in-it-for-me? thinking." Shaq himself admits that he didn't play especially well himself in the early going, but it wasn't entirely his fault. He wasn't getting the ball either. One NBA scout was shocked that in one game he observed,

O'Neal grew so frustrated as a junior when other teams got away with constantly fouling him, that he got embroiled in a fight with Carlos Groves (33) and Jay Price (10) of Tennessee. This game helped convince him to leave the college ranks a year early.

"Shaquille only touched the ball about twice in the entire second half."

To make things worse, rival coaches had learned that they could get away with aggressive tactics in defending Shaquille. "I had three and four defenders hanging on me every play," he said. "Coach Brown used to say that people were getting arrested out on the street for doing what they did to me on the basketball court."

It was becoming frustrating for Shaquille, who knew that some thought his statistics should improve as much from his second to third season as they had from his first to second. "But now people expected me to . . . maybe average 50 points a game. But I went down to 24.1 and people called me a disappointment. You know what happened. On every play I got double-teamed, triple-teamed, quadruple-teamed, fouled, hacked, handcuffed, and assaulted. . . ."

For the most part Shaquille stayed cool and kept his temper under control—until the Tigers faced the University of Tennessee in the SEC tournament. During that game Shaquille, alone behind the defense and preparing to dunk, was brought down hard by a player named Carlos Groves, about whom he later said, "If they had a position for fouling and talking, he would've been All-American." When Groves wouldn't let him go after the hard foul, Shaquille fought to break Groves' grip and swung his elbow. Neither player threw a punch, but all around them fights started breaking out. Even Coach Brown was on the floor fighting. Shaquille and the team had let their frustration get the better of them, and the result was that Shaquille was suspended from the next game, which the Tigers lost to Kentucky.

The Tennessee game helped convince Shaquille to turn pro before his senior season. Still, he was able to go out on a positive note with an impressive performance at the NCAA tournament. He set a tournament record by blocking 11 shots in a first-round victory against Brigham Young University, and in the next game, he scored 36 points and pulled down 12 rebounds in a valiant losing effort against a very good team, Bob Knight's Indiana Hoosiers. For the season, he averaged 24.1 points and led the country in rebounds per game and blocked shots. Again a consensus first-team All-American, and SEC Player of the Year, he was the runner-up to Duke's Christian Laettner for the Naismith and Wooden Awards, both of which are awarded, by different groups of voters, to the best player in college basketball.

On April 3, immediately following the NCAA tournament, Shaq held a press conference at Baton Rouge to announce that he would be foregoing his senior year to make himself eligible for the NBA draft. "I played my heart out," he said at the conference. "This isn't a money thing. I was taught at a young age that if you're not having fun at something, then it's time to go."

5

A WHOLE NEW BALL GAME

"I would be lying if I said the basketball part at LSU worked out for me as well as I hoped," Shaquille said of his three years at Baton Rouge. He found it hard to accept that he had never taken his team to the Final Four and that he was leaving college before earning his degree, but, he said, his decision to leave "was like all the decisions I ever made—once I made them, I didn't look back, didn't second-guess myself."

At the age of twenty, after all, Shaquille was more inclined to look forward than to look back during the spring and summer of 1992, and he had much to look forward to. He was going to the NBA, and despite the availability of Christian Laettner and Alonzo Mourning, he was a sure bet to be the number one pick in the draft. When the Orlando Magic won the right to pick first in the lottery drawing in May, Orlando fans and team officials were ecstatic. Orlando

All the pro teams wanted Shaquille—but only the Magic got him.

General Manager Pat Williams elatedly held up a Magic jersey with Shaq's name on it for all to see. The ten other teams in the lottery—all of whom had also had Shaq jerseys printed up—went home disappointed.

Orlando was famous for its tourist sites, but one Magic official noted, "As great as Disney World and Sea World are, they're not something local people can identify with. It's hard to root for Disney World." So Shaquille pleased Orlando fans to no end by announcing that he was interested in "chillin' with Mickey (Mouse)." Shaq flew to Orlando the day after the draft and tickled the thousands who turned out to welcome him by putting on a pair of Mickey Mouse ears.

It was no easy task, however, for the Magic to sign Shaquille. In order to come up with enough money to pay him, the Magic had to restructure the contracts of some players, and trade others—including guard Sam Vincent and Shaq's old LSU teammate Stanley Roberts, voted by the fans the most popular Magic player the year before. Shaquille's contract was for an astounding amount of money—$40 million for seven years, the biggest rookie contract by far in any sport—but he could not sign the contract by himself. Because he had not yet turned 21, his mother had to sign as well.

The hype for Shaquille in his rookie season was unprecedented. Before the Magic's training camp started, Shaq was off to Las Vegas to film a commercial with John Wooden, the legendary coach of the UCLA Bruins, and former NBA greats Wilt Chamberlain, Bill Russell, Kareem Abdul-Jabbar and Bill Walton. The commercial was part of the huge endorsement deal he and agent Leonard Armato had worked out with

Reebok—just one of many marketing and licensing deals they had struck before the season began. Shaquille, with Armato's help, was able to line up endorsements before playing a single game that were rivaled only by Michael Jordan and his one-man marketing empire. The O'Neal/Armato team even created a Shaq logo and took out a copyright on his nickname, Shaq, and the phrase Shaq Attaq.

When it was time to train with the team, however, Shaq stopped thinking about anything but basketball and got serious about preparing for the upcoming season. In training camp, Shaquille was welcomed by Magic veterans Nick Anderson, Greg Kite, Donald Royal, Scott Skiles, and Jeff Turner, and became especially close with Dennis Scott, the former Georgia Tech star who quickly became, in Shaq's words, "the older brother I never had, someone to talk to and trust." For his new teammates there was no jealousy over Shaq's fame and riches—they saw him as a player who could turn the fran-

In 1992, in his first game as a pro, Shaq frustrated John Salley of the Miami Heat.

chise around.

The first and hardest lesson Shaq had to learn was how to deal with double-teams. The swarming zone defenses that frustrated Shaq in college were not allowed in the NBA. But the NBA's man-to-man defenses allowed defenders to come from anywhere on the court to double-team the man with the ball. If the player with the ball didn't anticipate where the double-team was coming from and pass quickly to the open man—or worse, ignored it and tried to bull his way through two or three defenders—an offensive foul or turnover was often the result.

Another adjustment was learning how to run the high pick-and-roll, a play where the center has to come out to the perimeter—far out of Shaq's accustomed territory—to set a screen on the opposing guard, and then roll to the basket after the guard drives around the screen. And he had to learn about what he came to call "VBs" or "veteran bumps"—the kinds of things NBA players get away with that aren't exactly legal, like hiding illegal hand contact from the referees and pulling on opponents' shirts. It was a lot to learn in a short time, and Shaq had to learn it while going through grueling conditioning practices.

Shaq was no ordinary rookie, though, and he had little difficulty in adjusting to the NBA's style of play. Just how quick a learner Shaquille was became evident in his first exhibition game against the Miami Heat. Rony Seikaly immediately tried to go straight at Shaq. Shaq swatted his first shot into the seats. John Salley then tried to come inside with the ball, but intimidated by Shaq's presence, wound up throwing it over the backboard. When play was stopped a short time later, Shaq recalled that teammate Scott Skiles walked over to Seikaly and said, "It's a whole new ball game, Rony."

A month later Shaquille was up against the Heat once again, only this time the game was for real.

In his first official game Shaq had 18 rebounds, the highest total in a rookie debut since 1974, to go along with 12 points and 3 blocks. While Shaq did have trouble with turnovers, committing 8 in the game, the Magic, led by the scoring of Anderson and Scott, beat the Heat and also won their next game against the Washington Bullets. Shaquille earned four consecutive Rookie of the Month Awards in the first four months of the season, all but assuring himself of winning Rookie of the Year honors before the season was half over.

Everywhere Shaquille went, the fans mobbed him, and opposing players and coaches expressed admiration for his game. Don Nelson, coach of the Golden State Warriors and a perceptive student of the game, said of him: "I was surprised to see he was that good and that polished. From what other people told me, I thought he would have some trouble offensively. I had no idea he'd score so much. Someday he's going to be the best center in the league. He's got all the tools."

Where Nelson saw gentleness to Shaq's game, Seattle SuperSonics coach George Karl saw something else, something he called "Larry Bird eyes." Shaq took it as the compliment it was intended to be, saying it meant he had "scary eyes that tell everybody I've come to play." Indiana Pacers coach Larry Brown pointed out that Shaquille's work ethic was excep-

With his tongue hanging out, a la Michael Jordan, Shaq rips down a rebound.

tional: "I respect guys who come every single day and try to win and bust their butts. He's that." And opposing players, like Mike Sanders of the Cleveland Cavaliers, expressed a common sentiment among NBA players—something approaching awe at the sheer power of Shaq's game: "The guy attacks the basket like no one I've ever seen. I want to see the guy who would think of attempting to block one of his dunks. I guarantee that he'd break your hand if you tried it."

Shaquille was a little surprised himself by how he was taking the league by storm, but not too surprised. Before the season he thought he "might average ten points and nine rebounds. But once I got off to a quick start I knew I could play in this league." He was enjoying the game, and made no secret of the fact that he was having a good time. "Let's put it this way," he wrote in his autobiography, "if I was a fan, I would come to see Shaquille O'Neal dunk. I would also come to see him block shots. I'm not gonna lie. Sometimes I'm out there playing to the crowd. A quick smile, a wink. Yeah, I guess I'm showing off."

There were some players, however, who were slow to express admiration for the rookie who was getting all the attention. Patrick Ewing was particularly displeased to be beaten out by Shaq for the starting spot on the All-Star team, and others such as Karl Malone, who called him "just another player," were clearly somewhat resentful of Shaquille's instantaneous success and recognition. Furthermore, some held the opinion that Shaq was nothing but an amazing physical specimen, that his game was all brute strength and no finesse, and that all he could do was dunk. Not unfamiliar with this line of criticism, Shaquille recalled what an opposing coach had said when he was asked about Shaquille's lack of a pet shot. The coach, Brendan Suhr, had replied simply, "A dunk's a pretty good pet shot."

Perhaps the most exciting highlight of Shaq's rookie season was a nationally televised triple-overtime duel against Patrick Ewing and the Knicks just a week before the All-Star Game. Shaq and Patrick were both giving their all to show who was the best center in the Eastern Conference. Ewing wanted to prove the fans wrong for choosing the rookie to start in his place, and Shaq was equally determined to jus-tify their votes. Both players had a terrific game. While Shaquille had early foul trouble and was outscored by Ewing, 34 to 21, it was Ewing who fouled out of the game. Shaquille for his part dominated in the paint, just missing a triple double with 19 rebounds and 9 blocked shots. Two of the blocks preserved a tie for the Magic— one at the end of regulation and another at the end of the second overtime—and yet another, on Herb Williams at the end of the third overtime, iced the epic game for the Magic. The Knicks clamored for a goaltending call on Shaq to no avail. When asked about it after the game, Shaq

Shaq rapped with the group Fu-Schnickens during a 1992 appearance on the "Arsenio Hall Show."

said coolly and memorably, "I'm a shot blocker, not a goaltender."

Shaq won Rookie of the Year honors by getting 96 out of a possible 98 votes. The second place finisher was Alonzo Mourning of the Charlotte Hornets, whose outstanding season was completely eclipsed by the Shaq's outstanding season. The only NBA player to rank in the top ten in four categories, Shaq was second in rebounding, second in blocked shots, fourth in field goal percentage, and eighth in scoring. And yes, he did lead the league in the Shaq Attacks, with 270 slam dunks, one broken basket support, and a shattered backboard.

During the stretch drive, Shaquille had no problems with what is known as "the rookie wall," in which first-year players, used to a college schedule of 30 or so games, run out of steam at the tail end of the NBA's grueling schedule—81 games, not counting exhibitions or the playoffs. But Shaquille finished the season almost as strongly as he had started it. More important, he had kept the Magic in playoff contention for the entire season. They improved by 20 wins from the previous year to finish at 41 and 41, tied with the Indiana Pacers for the last playoff spot in the Eastern Conference.

Because they had won the season series, however, the Pacers advanced to the playoffs. The Magic's consolation was that they had improved so dramatically, and that they had a slim, one-in-sixty-six chance to get a second consecutive number one pick in the collegiate draft. Remarkably, that was all they needed. The Magic beat the odds and with the number one pick chose Chris Webber out of the University of Michigan. Within hours of choosing Webber, Pat Williams traded him to the Golden State Warriors for Anfernee "Penny" Hardaway, a 6'7" point guard from Memphis State University, and three future number one draft choices. Now Magic fans had good reason to begin thinking in terms of an NBA dynasty.

6
BUILDING A HOUSE ON LEGENDS LANE

Between his first and second NBA seasons, Shaquille was the Most Valuable Player on the gold medal-winning United States team in the World Championships of Basketball, but he attracted more attention with his activities off the court, which included recording a rap album, Shaq Diesel, that sold over a million copies, and appearing in the movie "Blue Chips" with Nick Nolte and his Magic teammate-to-be Anfernee Hardaway. He also went on two Reebok-sponsored tours, one to Europe and the other to Australia, Singapore, and Japan, where riot police had to be called in to protect him from adoring fans.

As he had done in his first year, Shaq had no trouble putting aside the distractions of the off-season once the Magic began playing. The team was vastly improved in 1993-94, rising to a fifty-win season, placing them among the league's elite. While their improvement owed much to Penny Hardaway, who was showing that he, like

In 1995, Shaq got to match his skills against the center he respected the most, Hakeem Olajuwon, in the NBA Finals.

Shaq, needed very little time to establish himself as an impact player in the NBA, the more important fact was that Shaq was again surpassing all expectations. He was taking more shots, and making more shots, and only a 72-point performance on the last day of the season by David Robinson of the San Antonio Spurs kept Shaq from winning the NBA scoring title. Shaq was again second in the league in rebounding, sixth in blocked shots, and for the second year in a row he was the only player in the top ten in four categories.

The ultimate indicator of how much Shaq's game had improved was not his individual statistics, but that the Magic had improved by another nine victories to clinch a high seed in the playoffs. With the playoffs, however, the Magic's season came to a crashing thud. Up against the Indiana Pacers, the Eastern Conference's hottest team for the second half of the season, the Magic failed to win even a single game in their best of five series. Pacer guards Reggie Miller and Byron Scott beat them with clutch outside shooting and the Pacers' interior defense, with Derrick McKey, 7'4" Rik Smits, Antonio Davis, and Dale Davis, did an effective job on Shaq, holding him to a season-low 15 points in the second game and to nearly nine points below his average for the series. The Magic were devastated by the loss, and Shaq in particular was beside himself after the series. "He took a lot of it on his shoulders," said Dennis Scott. He felt that he, as the team leader, had let the Magic down.

Shaq came back for the 1994-95 season determined not to let the same thing happen again. "I'm smarter," he said. "I have a few more moves down low, and I'm stronger and quicker. Every year I've tried to get better at certain things." For his third season, he had added a baby hook shot to his repertoire and seemed more willing than ever to spin to the baseline to take—and make—a twelve- to fourteen-foot jumper in the manner of his friend Hakeem Olajuwon. To go with his new array of finesse moves, Shaquille sported a new look as well—a Superman tattoo on his left arm. Not everyone could get away with such a bold display of self-confidence, but if anyone was becoming Superman in the league, it was indeed Shaq. In fact in a poll of 21 NBA coaches taken before the season, nine of them chose Shaquille "as the player you would take first if you were starting a franchise."

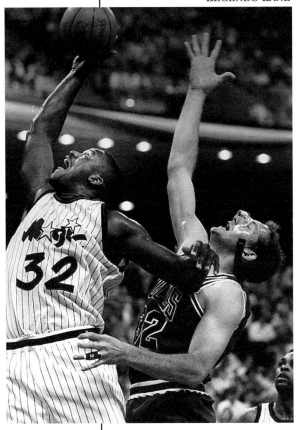

Will Perdue of Chicago has no chance of stopping Shaq in the 1995 playoffs.

At the halfway point of the season, the Magic were well represented at the All-Star Game in Phoenix. Shaquille started at center, Penny at guard, and Brian Hill, Orlando's coach, was at the helm of the Eastern team. Shaquille had a 22-point, 7-rebound performance and even took a three-pointer, as he had vowed he would do in previous games. Unfortunately, it fell a couple of feet short of the rim.

Shaquille had an excellent opportunity to showcase how much his game had improved against the league's best in one week in March, when he had to play Patrick Ewing at home on a Tuesday and then go on the road to face

Hakeem Olajuwon on Thursday and David Robinson on Friday—something he characterized as a stroll down Legends Lane. After Shaquille played as well as or better than each of the three future Hall of Fame centers in leading the Magic to two wins and a tough last-second one-point loss, *Sports Illustrated* wrote that "it was more obvious than ever that O'Neal not only deserves to reside on Legend's Lane, but he also soon will have the biggest house on the block."

Every season brings its small controversies, and this one was no exception, starting with the awarding of the MVP trophy. Many thought Shaq deserved the award and with a month to go in the season, he seemed to have it locked up. But thanks to some terrible foul-shooting problems at year's end and a late-season slide by the Magic—and a run by the Spurs—David Robinson came away with it.

Still, aside from some work on his free throws, there was nothing else anyone could have asked of him in just his third year in the league. Again he was in the top ten in the four most important categories for a center—in addition to winning the scoring crown by a comfortable margin, he was second in field goal percentage, third in rebounding, and sixth in blocked shots. More important, he led his team to exactly where they wanted to be—by finishing first in the Eastern Conference, they enjoyed the home-court advantage against all their conference opponents and, as it turned out, throughout the entire playoffs.

Michael Jordan returned to the Chicago Bulls, but, to the surprise of the entire basketball world, that too proved to be somewhat of an anticlimax. The second-round series pitting the Bulls against the Magic looked to be a dream matchup—the Shaq vs. Air Jordan—and indeed there was a good deal of high drama in the series, especially after Nick Anderson of the Magic had told the press that "45's not 23," implying that Jordan was not the same player he once was. An angry Jordan defied league rules by changing his jersey number from 45 back to his old 23 and set out to teach the young upstarts a lesson. For a while it looked as though Chicago's experience and their Hack-a-Shaq defense (using a rotation of three centers to foul Shaq at every opportunity) would prevail. But it was the poised play of the youngsters from Orlando down the stretch of key games, and an even more surprising series of last-minute miscues by Jordan, that gave the series to the Magic, four games to two.

After avenging their previous year's early playoff exit by overcoming the Pacers in a thrilling seven-game series, the Magic were one of two teams left standing in a final-round matchup no one could have foreseen. Despite the Magic's conference championship, basketball pundits thought the veteran squads from Indiana, Chicago, or New York would come out of the East on top, but Houston's winning the West was an even bigger surprise. Absolutely no one—except or course perhaps themselves—thought the Rockets would survive until the final round.

Facing a steady stream of injury problems and personality conflicts, Houston's play in the regular season was sporadic at best, and many felt the midseason trade of power forward Otis Thorpe for Hakeem's old college teammate Clyde

Drexler, a guard, was a mistake. On paper, it made the Rockets, the league's worst rebounding team to start with, even more vulnerable in their weakest area. But Drexler's leadership turned out to be a major intangible and he was a huge asset throughout the playoffs. The Rockets won road series in three of the toughest arenas in the league—Utah, Phoenix, and San Antonio—before they arrived at the O-Rena, where the Magic had been virtually impossible to beat the entire season.

The series did not last long. Fans of the Magic are still playing a game of "what if?" when they remember the way the Rockets swept their heroes in four straight games. What if, they wonder, the Magic had not let a 20-point lead slip away in Game 1? And what if Nick Anderson had made just one of four free throws in a ten-second span to ice what still looked like a certain victory? He didn't—the Rockets won Game 1 in overtime, and the Magic never recovered.

While Hakeem was clearly the star of the series, it was the excellent play of Houston's role players like Sam Cassell, Robert Horry, and Mario Elie, coupled with disappointing series from Anderson, Hardaway, Dennis Scott, and Horace Grant, that made the difference in the Finals. The head-to-head matchup between the two great centers was, in fact, statistically quite close. Hakeem, with his deadly array of moves and spins, had the edge in scoring by nearly five points per game, but he found it difficult to control his counterpart's low-post game—Shaq still scored 28 points a game, and tallied more rebounds, more blocks, and had a much higher shooting percentage from the floor than

Hakeem.

But Hakeem was the dominant player when it counted most. When the Rockets needed a key basket or rebound he got it, and his blocked shots at important junctures always seemed to lead to crowd-awakening fast-break dunks or three-pointers. The Rockets could take risks on defense knowing they had the best defensive center in the league behind them to protect the basket. Shaq could be proud of the way he played, but Hakeem controlled this series as he had every postseason series he had played in for the past two years.

When Horace Grant tried to help out Shaq, Olajuwon hit the open man. Hakeem played spectacularly as the Houston Rockets won their second championship in a row. Shaq did all he could—but his first championship is still in the future.

After the season he was not only off to play a rapping genie in a new film, he also planned to grant his mother's wish and return to LSU to work on finishing his college degree. In one remarkable commercial for a soft drink Shaq was shown to be an all-American hero who transcends his time. Using sophisticated technology the ad had Shaq riding a horse with the Cartwright brothers in the old TV series "Bonanza," appearing with 1950s comedians Lucille Ball and Jackie Gleason, and walking on the moon with the Apollo 11 crew. He has also found a television comedy partner in Hakeem, with whom he appeared in another celebrated series of spots—the two giants dressed as little boys in white shorts and bow ties, riding a tandem bicycle together or floating down a lazy river.

The 1994-95 season was the closest that O'Neal would ever get to winning the NBA finals with the Magic. He broke his thumb in the next preseason and missed Orlando's first 22 games, although the Magic still ended the 1995-96 regular season atop the Atlantic Division with a 60-22 record. Orlando then eliminated the Detroit Pistons and the Atlanta Hawks in the first two rounds of the playoffs before getting swept by the Chicago Bulls, the eventual NBA champions, in the Eastern Conference finals.

Orlando's final playoff loss to the Bulls, on May 27, marked Shaquille's last appearance in a Magic uniform. A free agent as soon as the season ended, he found himself in the middle of an incredible bidding war between Orlando and the Los Angeles Lakers. He eventually rejected the Magic's offer in favor of a Laker contract worth well over $100 million. Then, with the ink on his new deal barely dry, he helped lead the U.S. Olympic basketball team to a gold medal at the Atlanta Olympics.

Shaquille's departure from Orlando meant that the Magic would never become the basketball dynasty that many people had predicted it would. But his arrival in Los Angeles meant that the Lakers, with their rich history of Hall-of-Fame centers (namely, George Mikan, Wilt Chamberlain, and Kareem Abdul-Jabbar), might one day be adding a new chapter to their NBA legend.

CHRONOLOGY

1972   Born in Newark, New Jersey

1989   Leads Cole High School to undefeated Texas State Championship season; named to *Parade* magazine's High School All-America Team and is selected as MVP in two national all-star games

1991   Named National Collegiate Player of the Year by the Associated Press, United Press International, and *Sports Illustrated*

1992   Signs with Orlando Magic after being first player chosen in the draft; is named Player of Week in his first week in the league

1993   Wins Rookie of the Month Award his first four months in the league; wins Rookie of the Year honors with 96 out of a possible 98 first-place votes; is only NBA player to rank in top ten in four categories (scoring, field goal percentage, rebounding, blocked shots); becomes youngest player ever chosen to play in NBA All-Star Game and the first rookie starter since Michael Jordan;

        Wins gold medal representing United States at the World Championships of Basketball and is chosen Tournament MVP; stars in the film *Blue Chips* and records million-selling rap album, *Shaq Diesel*

1994   Finishes second in the NBA in scoring, first in field-goal percentage, and second in rebounding; takes Orlando to their first playoffs

1995   Leads the NBA in scoring, and is second in field goal percentage, third in rebounds, and sixth in blocked shots; is close runner-up in MVP voting; leads Orlando to the Eastern Conference title

1996   Signs with the Los Angeles Lakers; wins a gold medal with "Dream Team III" at the Atlanta Olympics

STATISTICS

SHAQULLE O'NEAL

SEASON	TEAM	G	FGA	FGM	PCT	FTA	FTM	PCT	RBD	AST	PTS	AVG
1989-90	LSU	32	314	180	.573	153	85	.556	385	61	445	13.9
1990-91	LSU	28	497	312	.628	235	150	.638	411	45	774	27.6
1991-92	LSU	30	478	294	.615	254	134	.528	421	46	722	24.1
Totals		90	1289	786	.610	642	369	.575	1217	152	1941	21.6

SEASON	TEAM	G	FGA	FGM	PCT	FTA	FTM	PCT	RBD	AST	PTS	AVG
1992-93	Orl	81	1304	733	.562	721	427	.592	1122	152	1893	23.4
1993-94	Orl	81	1491	**953**	**.599**	850	471	.554	1072	195	2377	29.3
1994-95	Orl	79	**1594**	**930**	.583	854	455	.533	901	214	**2315**	**29.3**
1995-96	Orl	54	1033	592	.573	511	249	.487	596	155	1434	26.6
Totals		295	5522	3208	.581	2936	1602	.546	3691	716	8019	27.2

bold indicates league-leading figures

G	games
FGA	field goals attempted
FGM	field goals made
PCT	percent
FTA	free throws attempted
FTM	free throws made
RBD	rebounds
AST	assists
PTS	points
AVG	scoring average

SUGGESTIONS FOR FURTHER READING

Bjarkman, Peter C. *Shaq: The Making of a Legend.* New York: Smithmark, 1994.

Gutman, Bill. *Shaquille O'Neal: A Biography.* New York: Archway Paperbacks, 1993.

O'Neal, Shaquille, with Jack McCallum. *Shaq Attaq!* New York: Hyperion, 1993.

White, Ellen Emerson. *Shaquille O'Neal.* New York: Scholastic, Inc., 1994.

ABOUT THE AUTHOR

A native of Minneapolis, MN, Tim Ungs received English degrees from the University of Notre Dame (BA) and the University of Minnesota (MA). He worked at HarperCollins Publishers in New York in publicity and marketing for five years—most recently as an in-house copywriter for the Adult Trade Division. Currently he is a freelance writer and a World Wide Web consultant. He lives in Brooklyn, NY, with his wife and dog.

INDEX

Abdul-Jabbar, Kareem, 11, 22, 44
Anderson, Kenny, 35
Anderson, Nick, 45, 47, 57, 58
Arkansas State University, 37
Armato, Leonard, 44-45
"Arsenio Hall Show," 50
Ball, Lucille, 60
Barkley, Charles, 12, 16, 36
Bird, Larry, 9, 11-12, 47
Blue Chips, 53
Boston Celtics, 36
Bowie, Sam, 15
Brigham Young University, 41
Brown, Dale, 23, 30, 40, 41
Brown, Larry, 47
Carse, Craig, 30, 35
Cassell, Sam, 58
Chamberlain, Wilt, 22, 44
Chicago Bulls, 10, 57
Cowens, Dave, 22
Davis, Antonio, 54
Davis, Dale, 54
Davis, Marcia, 19
Dawkins, Darryl, 14
Drexler, Clyde, 16, 58
Dumars, Joe, 60
Durham, Hugh, 38
Elie, Mario, 58
Erving, Julius, 11
Ewing, Patrick, 10, 14, 16-17, 48,
    49, 55
Gathers, Hank, 35
Georgia Tech, 35
Gleason, Jackie, 60
Grant, Horace, 58, 59
Groves, Carlos, 40-41
Gutman, Bill, 26
Hardaway, Anfernee, 51, 53-54,
    55, 58
Harrison, Lucille O'Neal, 19-20,
    26-27, 28, 44, 60

Harrison, Philip, 20-22-23, 27,
    31, 33, 39
Hill, Brian, 55
Horry, Robert, 58
Houston Rockets, 57-59
Indiana Pacers, 50, 54, 57
Indiana University, 41
Jackson, Chris, 34-35, 36, 37
Johnson, Larry, 13, 16, 35
Johnson, Magic, 9, 11-12, 13
Johnson, Melvin, 38
Jordan, Michael, 9-10, 11-12, 13,
    14, 15, 16, 45, 56-57
Karl, George, 47
Kite, Greg, 45
Laettner, Christian, 33, 41, 43
Laimbeer, Bill, 37
Louisiana State University, 19,
    30-31, 33-41, 43
Loyola Marymount University, 35
McKey, Derrick, 54
McNeese State University, 38
Madura, Dave, 26
Malone, Karl, 14, 16, 17, 48
Mashburn, Jamal, 38
Miami Heat, 46-47
Mickey Mouse, 44
Miller, Reggie, 54
Mills, Chris, 37
More, Herb, 26, 27, 28
Mourning, Alonzo, 43, 50
Nelson, Don, 47
New York Knicks, 49
Olajuwon, Hakeem, 14, 16, 53,
    55, 56, 58-59, 60
O'Neal, Shaquille
    as a performer, 13, 20, 44, 48,
    50, 53, 60
    honors received, 12, 15, 17, 30,
    39, 41, 50, 53
    injuries of, 38

Orlando Magic, 43-51, 53-60
Perdue, Will, 55
Pippen, Scottie, 16
Price, Jay, 40
Riley, Pat, 16-17
Roberts, Stanley, 34, 36, 44
Robertson, Oscar, 22
Robinson, David, 14, 16, 54, 56
Rooks, Sean, 37
Royal, Donald, 45
Russell, Bill, 22, 44
Salley, John, 45, 46
Sanders, Mike, 48
Scott, Byron, 54
Scott, Dennis, 35, 45, 54, 58
Seikaly, Rony, 15, 46-47
Skiles, Scott, 45, 47
Smits, Rik, 54
Stockton, John, 16, 17
Suhr, Brendan, 49
Thomas, Isiah, 16
Thorpe, Otis, 57
Turner, Jeff, 45
University of Arizona, 37
University of Connecticut, 38
University of Georgia, 38
University of Kentucky, 38, 41
University of Nevada, Las Vegas,
    35
University of Tennessee, 40, 41
Unseld, Wes, 22
Villanova University, 35
Vincent, Sam, 44
Walton, Bill, 36, 44
Webber, Chris, 51
West, Jerry, 22
Wilkins, Dominique, 27
Williams, Brian, 37
Williams, Herb, 49
Williams, Pat, 51
Wooden, John, 44

PICTURE CREDITS
AP/Wide World Photos: pp. 2, 10, 13, 40, 42, 45, 48, 50, 52, 55, 59; Reuters/Bettmann: pp. 8, 14; Courtesy Marcia Davis: p. 18; UPI/Bettmann: p. 20; Courtesy Louisiana State University: pp. 22, 32, 37; Lynne Dobson/Austin-American Statesman: pp. 24, 29.